The Breaking
No Love - Poems of Shadows and Survival

Shanita Menso

Copyright © 2025 Shanita Menso. All rights reserved.

No part of this book may be reproduced, distributed, or transmitted in any form or by any means without the prior written permission of the author, except in brief quotations used in reviews or academic work. Images contained within are AI generated in collaboration with the writer.

Published by Truly Rooted Press Allentown, PA 18103

ISBN (Paperback): 979-8-9938969-2-2

U.S. Copyright Registration Pending.

For the child I was,
for the children misplaced through no fault of their own,
and for every survivor still learning to breathe and accept themselves.

TABLE of CONTENTS

Acknowledgements   i

I. FRACTURES & FALLING

Sinking	1
Road Closed	3
IDK	4
A Dimming	5
My Empty	7
In October	8
Her Weight	10
Ghost of a Home	11

II. ECHOES OF ABANDONMENT

You left.	12
Dear Mother	13
Dragon's Ransom	15
The Hardest Thing	17
Transitory	18
Love- Find me	19
Friendly Hope	20
Echoes of My Frame	21

III. LONGING

Stranger	22
Tucked Away	23
Caged	25
Toy	26
I Heard	27
Hunger for Love	29
Shadow Tells a Story	30

Give it a title	33
Mask	34

IV. CAPTIVITY

Stole, from me	35
Backstabbed	36
In Bondage	37
Warped Family	39
Me?	40
Bathroom Brushes	41
Trash Bag Queen	42
Twisted	43
Hit Me	44
Down Eyes	45
Let's See	46

V. RESIDUE & REACHING

Uneasily Demised?	47
Littlest Page	48
Breathless	49
My Plea	50
Flicker	51
Their Rockin' Robin	52
Liminal	53
Raccoon's Goodbye	54
Bright Eyes	56
Sublime	57
Lost Passion	59
Will I find me?	60
Recollection	61
Inescape	62
Unfair Trade	63
Control Is Not Love	64

VI. COLLAPSE & CLARITY

The Storm	67
Not a Dream	69
Quake	70
Hollow Child	71
Tangent Maze	73
Generations, One Dream	75
First Race XC	77
Perfection	79
Family	81
Celebrated	83
Capsized	84
Depleated	85
Breaking	86
Unmothered	87

ABOUT THE AUTHOR

ACKNOWLEDGMENTS

This first part of the trilogy, written between 2006 and 2010 when I was fourteen through nineteen, is composed of poems that were never reread or edited after being written– with the exception of punctuation and spelling. They served as an emotional release, and at the time I believed revisiting them would undo the purpose of putting them on paper. I stumbled upon many of my journals and began reading them recently, and feel that sharing my experiences from childhood may help others understand preteens and teens who were in similar situations. I want to specifically thank all the teachers who allowed me to stay longer to study, nap, and even ask them the thousands of questions that came to my mind during my inquisitive years. I extend my deepest gratitude to the school counselors and assigned counselors who, for a brief time in my childhood, held space for me with courage and steadiness. Thank you for sitting with me and allowing me in the moments when existence was painful, and presence itself was the most powerful form of care.

To the caseworkers and county workers –specifically one with silver hair, another with silly socks, and the third with bucket seats and thick accent– who guided me through the many crossings of my life—your diligence, advocacy, and commitment shaped perspective in ways unimaginable. Each of you, in your own way, helped build the framework through which I learned resilience, safety, and voice.

To the foster families who received me, with gentleness and intentions imperfect, I acknowledge the lessons you offered. Some of you showed me what love could look like; others taught me what love should never be, and my family, Your presence shaped me. I recognize that every person who appeared in my journey could only meet me from the place they stood in their own lives. I am grateful for those who showed up with the capacities they had, even when they themselves were in need.

To the children who, like me, lived/live in places not of their choosing—your existence continues to remind me of the strength born from displacement and the quiet hope that persists despite uncertainty.

And finally, to all who have shared even a small portion of their humanity with me—whether through guidance, random conversations in laundry mats park benches, and bus stops, even in conflict; Thank you for sharing your unique me perspective that helped in shaping my understanding of this lived human experience.

The Breaking

Sinking

(Originally Titled: _The Sinking of a Gender_)
For every tear you've seen fall from my eyes-
There have been millions behind closed doors.
I have grown afraid of who I was because
I saw she scared you.
I saw the old me make older women cry and
feel ashamed of their behavior.
I have seen the old me give one look and snap an attitude into order.
Drop a person creating drama in a heartbeat
Drop pretend friends like flies.
Tell the truth to your face and have someone in shock
 count it as a lie.
She gave three chances and three only.
Walked tall and not look back.
She moved with the swiftness of the wind
Navigated life with the slyness of a fox
Yet, for you I put her in a box.
She scared you.
I saw that she made you nervous,
 Made the women around you uneasy.
She took no prisoners
And spared none from the truth.
Her power and strength literally pulled hearts to their graves.
I scared you, and so I locked myself away.
Each compromise I gave for love
was brick adding to a jail cell.
 Every cut short argument stitch designed to
silence me.

Every blind eye I turned, an extra lock to the door.
I compromised myself for your love
And all you did was ask for and require more.

My entire life I have been taught :
That I am not my own.
My body is not a temple but a belonging
My opinion and my voice don't matter.
Beat down by those who were intimidated
by the young but strong woman they saw before them.
In the end the prison guard was me.

I believed all of the lies fed to me.
You're not fit to be a human,
Not worthy of love,
Property of _____
A belonging to_____
I thrived on a diet of lies.
Then a few days ago I opened my eyes.

I once opened my mouth and life came out.
The sky lit up the night for me
My womb bore fruit as if a tree
And gave life.
My, how Magical and mystical I must be....

I once spoke healing into the sick
Halted quicksand with the swipe of my hand
And brought down a mighty fortress with a single kiss
I lit up the sky with my laughter
Loved without limits
And lived and praised as if it was the last time I would ever.
I was once one with myself, and she with me.

But I boxed her up for shallow promises
and broken dreams.
Today I chose to set her free.
No longer I wish
A prisoner of my own choosing.

Road Closed

Red flags "turn around don't come this way"
But I carry on through my day.
Caution signs flash and light up signs appear
"Turn back young lady don't venture here"
I followed the road
No happiness gained
I just lost myself.
Strong wounded woman trying as hard as she can
To recover from the accident caused by curiosity and love.
I never knew such a struggle.

"How will this road treat me?"
Turn back they all say
The pavers and natives say the road is still young and wry.
While you still remember your way,
Go back and gain strength to journey someplace new.
"Ignore them" the pavement says beneath my feet.
"Follow me, I will make your life complete."

As I explore the path before my steps
A noticeable gap appears in the road.
No way around it, and no bridge to cross
I leap over the obstacle in the name of love.
The road whispers to me sweet woes and despair
And I fall to my knees due to shortness of air.
"cuidado!!!" Says the road block before my face
Still onward I travel.
Many obstacles later a voice gallantly states
"THIS ROAD IS CLOSED"
Eyes open, my back turns away.
To the roads start I return to travel another day.

IDK

My current position remains undefined,
The intricacies of my perspective pervade me.
Heart's position ambiguously drawn,
And the demarcation between rectitude and error
unclear.
But in the chaos, still I
perceive,
a current of serenity runs through
recollections.
Although much remains obscure,
this verity endures:
Persevere, we'll get through.

A Dimming

Everyone says "Look at that girl"
Look at her smile-
The pearls light up the ocean floor-
Here I stand-smile welcoming a friend-
Arms open to greet-
Eyes see what no one else sees-
the need for a hug.
Always hearing… never interfering
with the connection between the two.
Bouts and brawls -
spouts and falls
Only lending my advice when asked-
Reaching out when there is an opening-
I am here to comfort- here to listen attentive as always
For I will always be the lending shoulder and ear
Wanted someone to hear.

There is nothing binding there for you
 No marriage vows-no children-

No obligation to stay and love.
But is it love?
Ranting and raving- paranoid about "the prize"
I see a person worth saving-no property is he.
First it's looks- then its lies
Precious time this girl buys-
But no- not bought for it was given
No remorse for the heart that's slowly breaking.

The Eyes that used to glitter-
 No longer glisten.
the smile lit like the sun-
 barely peaks out from the clouds
 Small snippets of time to share only this allowed.
 New friendship no longer able to keep -
 buried with the plow from days of old.

Kept under control from stories told
Unable to express free thought
without that feeling of betrayal.

Everyone says "See at that girl,"
Look at her eyes –
The stars that light up the night
Giving that hint of concern
The plight for freedom-
The cry for his star-
That danced like the northern lights
But no longer moves to the music of life.
Controlled by the one he called wife
New scrapes and bruises–
New scars to hide
this done by the hands of his radiant bride.
Who ever told the tale that men don't cry
Drown it in the depths of the deepest sea
It's a lie!

I was the friend who saw him cry
I was the one who dried his eyes
I was the one who iced his sprains-
quelled his temper- put out flames.
Mine were the ears attentive to his plea-
Mine were the lips that cautioned "flee"
But he cried love-and ignored me
If he had run-still here he'd be
And I'd watch the stars dance across his face
but at least now from her I know he's safe.

-So, Be that friend-

My Empty

Ms. Do right-Ms. Prim and Proper
The only one who made it out
Now I look back.
I want what they have,
happiness.
They possess something I've only pretended-
Freedom.

I see the joy they have in their lives
While mine remains empty
I've plateaued on this level of "ok"
All others climb to great.
They were my tutored-
My unforgettable friends,relatives, companions
But what good is schooling
when my goal in life is unwritten.

The sacrifices of time, money, and sanity
To gain but one ounce of accomplishment-
When my only goal in life was to love and be loved
To live, thrive, and be happy.
With all I've lived through and all I see in front of
The vision of myself is as clear as this glass...
EMPTY.

What good is life without taking chances-
Without taking risks
Without becoming vulnerable?
It has the same value of a heart that does not beat.

Ms. Play it safe steps off of the sideline of life-
I'm still not ready for my turn-
But this body holds a passion for which I deeply yearn.
A hunger I have witnessed deep within these eyes-
For passion and excitement he'll indulge in all his life.
wonder what eyes see when they look at me-
Have they by chance glimpsed at this yearning -

Or do they see my EMPTY?

In October

You're one of a kind, you know.
You inspired and lit a flame in me.
I was terrified but desperately didn't know how deeply
I needed to be seen.
Soft sorrowful brown eyes.
Joyful yet blues-filled shy smile.
Raspy laughter—like a lit match—you made me
forget…

Dare I stay here hiding in the fort,
drinking Mexican hot chocolate,
looking at your artwork,
and talking about your dreams
and hopeful future happenings.

So innocent, yet hushed by this pattern of loss.
I sometimes search for you in the madness of it all,
hoping you don't slip.
Grab my hand, memories, and don't let go.

Robbing time blind—
and it's what I'd do for this soulful connection.

Manhunt in the park,
talking about all of life's unfortunate turns,
about the things we want to achieve when grown.

Skateboarding, breakdancing, turning away.
No choices given to stay!
I apologize for my leave—
any woes left in my waking.

Remember, sweet soul–

Your life is yours for the taking.
I hope I remember your face and your voice
Hope to see you in the future living your dream.

Her Weigh

I'll always love you.
I know so many people—
My siblings included—
Will blame you for so many many things.

I've heard I'm a drinker or smoker
—because she's an addict,
I can't love well because
I didn't know a mother's love.
I heard them all plain as day,
Spew all the nasty things they'd say
For the girl forced into womanhood
Who reluctantly bore fruit—
And bore more weight
than young shoulders should
You labored for us all.

I'd cut in to their speaking
let them know how I see you,
Beautifully broken, fighting unseen war
Kindness overflowing from a heart overburdened
So maybe they'll all understand a little more:
That you did all you could.

You chewed our food.
You brushed our teeth.
Took as best care you knew
Until you snapped from loss—
And we all lost you.

I can imagine the pain you carried
Seeing those you love
dead and buried,
Forced to accept the abuses you endured
At the hand of the family that should have loved you,
So you could love each of the fruit. . .
      Who were torn from your branches.

Ghost of a Home

I remember you saying I should have been aborted.
  Then the times you trailed me with dangled promises—
  "I've got a place for us," you said, "we'll be together soon."
  I know you meant it in your heart, but your lips told lies.

How could you promise to love me
  when you only know how to leave?
  In the suffocating emptiness you left behind,
  there is barely room to breathe.

You left.
  They left.
  I was never chosen; unseen lingers—
  I'm left in this deafening alone.
  We can't be together when you never learned
  to have a loving home.

You left.

This kind of deep pang
This hollow empty thing—
Is what you left.

When you left you took my laughter.
took my smile.
took my abuser with you–
But she and you are the same.

I love imperfectly, I love unsure,
I see your struggles and imperfections—
And I love you even more.
Still you left.

You would expect me to be mad,
Oddly I am slightly glad
Leaving was likely your only choice
Since no one listened to your raspy voice
How unkind to be unwanted and unseen

You left.
Passing on your gift of woundedness in invisibility.

Dear Mother

You didn't deserve them forcing womanhood on you,
You didn't deserve to be sold as only a body worth,
You didn't deserve to be beaten, mistreated, disrespected, used,
abused or put aside.
I know and see your pain
See behind the facade
And why behind these substances you hide.

You're not alone.
Even before I was a thought,
50% of my being existed within you.

Your strength and tenacity,
Your rough and confusing tone—
That joyful glow you glow even in sadness—
These things I know are all you.

The way you provided as best you could,
While people judged and no one else understood...
I see the kindness you bestow
those who wanted to absorb your glow.
Everyone's angle and everyone's show...
It's finally time you accept fully and know:

Mother—you are loved.
You are wanted beyond measure.

We cried so many nights for you,
Hoping for the day you'd realize you're worthy
to accept love's treasures.
I know this world feels like it's got you broken,
But innocence stolen is no man's token
I know you've been picked up, tossed around, clowned,
Dipped on, ghosted, by this world deeply tested
then all kinds of arrested...

I know you did the best you knew to do
In the time and capacity of the hand you were dealt.
I can't imagine how isolating and alone that felt.
But each step and beat,

You carry a piece of all of them, and of me.
So never alone you'd have to be.
Even if abused and confused towards us
Even warped and twisted convoluted love.
No one taught you love's meaning.

Your pain carries shock waves.
Your absence—a vacancy only He can fill.
Still, you are loved.

You left.
You made choices, you see.
I have to put down boundaries—
I can't let your demons overpower me!
Or let you determine who I am to Me
So while all your actions and choices somehow punished,
I define who I should step forth to be.
You left.
I am.
Still, you are loved.

Dragon's Ransom

An egg hatched in motherless nest,
raised by the elements.
She learned to survive,
self-sufficient, yet needing of rest.

Was taken into new nests,
none well fitted with love,
none trustworthy enough.
All the mothers who tasked to set out for young scales
showed to her their horns.

Misplaced blame, she digested—
left by siblings whose misdeeds
infested hearts to rot against the hatchling.

Nothing to explore
kept in empty rooms
locked door.
The ants her only friend.

Seldom birthday remembrance,
Little holiday cheer;
No food,
no fresh air—
only fun of pretend.

No one left honest,
 and her heart hinges beginning to rust—
Small voice tilled on heavy air
singing in whispers Wade.

Poems and song to pass time,
names and plays danced out by claws and ants.

Locked away in empty room,

stench-filled air,
daylight viewed through veiled window—
each day filled with gloom.

Mothers called her filthy; her scales were darker than others.
She was called "dirty," forced to scrub her skin raw.

Closeted darkness,
deep hidden caverns under bed—
safest fantasy retreat.

The Hardest Thing

The hardest thing about living is—
mourning those you love.
No, I'm not talking 'bout the ones
called to the beyond.

It's the ones who are here,
loved ones who disappear.
It's the ones we hold close,
the silly ones we confide in the most.

The hardest thing is so perplexing—
how can you mourn if love's only forlorn?

Oh, I miss your smiles,
long to hear your laughter.
Hug you tightly in my arms now,
and forever after.

You're still here…
just not here, with me.

Transitory

Sometimes I place my hand on my chest in the center...
Here, I can feel my heart beating
I remind myself that I am allowed to be human too.
I close my eyes, and I can hear the hum all around me
Children calling their parents
The hustle and bustle outside my door–
All this makes me wonder
I think how small we are in this universe.
In society we are like ants always moving on a path–
Never halting long enough to really admire or enjoy
Pleasures of a single moment.

I plan to enjoy this life.

Love- Find me

Character shifts the lens—
it can change how we're seen.
I want the one who loves me
to look and say:
"It doesn't matter what you look like—
your light is bright.
It doesn't matter what you do—
I'll never stop loving you."

Let's paint walls,
rip up carpets and nails,
patch old holes,
and build something whole—
so my children learn
that love is best friends
choosing one another,
every day.

Am I wrong for wanting
a windfall of romance
that never runs dry?
The kind that stirs nephews and nieces
to dream of something more—
a love that outlives lifetimes.

I used to get lost
in the awe of the world
and forget to find myself
within it.
It's scary in here sometimes,
behind the smile—
but I've learned to listen
to the quiet truths beneath. Love find me.

Friendly Hope

I am unfinished.
I pray not to leave too much pain behind me,
too much silence where joy once lived.
I hope I'm walking toward a place
where emptiness cannot follow.

Search me and see:
even fragmented,
I've learned love still can exist
Brokenness taught me
shaped by the hands that dare to reach.
Absent parents still teach.

Maybe friendship is all it becomes.
Maybe it's more.
Maybe one day, it's you and me—
brave and healed—
side by side.

Until then,
as I walk where the wind carries me…
I hope I find kindness within a friend.

Echoes of My Frame

My faith is resounding
within the echoes of my frame.
I know my purpose,
and I know my Savior's name.

Still, as are you,
an unfinished work.

Stranger

You're not my mother,
  I'm just your responsibility.
  Can't say I want my mother—
  unsure if she even loves me.
She didn't teach me
  how to read or write or tie shoes.
  No hugs or kisses can replace
  a void or loss so cosmically large.
Memories of her face
  and the feel of her voice
  dance around me—
  I remember
  a low, soulful, sung tune.
I know I admire
  parts of who you are,
  but I'm always reminded
  I wasn't born from you or yours.
You're more harsh with me—
  mothers keeping food and meds away,
  forcing secrets so no one sees
  forced solitude or neglect.
A familiar place—
  for a home
  is all any child wishes for.
  But I'm an outsider,
  and you show me
  in gestures,
  in shallow performances
  still called love.
You keep saying
  you can't get rid of me.
  I know
  She isn't you.

Tucked Away

I got grounded.
Grounded for breathing.
Grounded for eating.
Grounded for asking.

Told I have to stay on the porch, so I did—
still the neighborhood kids speak to me.
Then grounded…
not allowed to step outside.
Pebbles from Angel, who spoke my name,
Tap-tap, outside the windowpane.
Was asked to bring food to a sister in need.

Snuck out,
got hit by a car,
ran scared, limping through hurts and bleeds.
Hid out of fear of being punished again—
Then grounded for sneaking out to give clothing, pads,
and food to a friend.

Grounded– feeling suffocated while still alive.
No slow death from bleeding wounds.
Stepped on my own tongue
to keep from speaking too soon.
Fell asleep in my closet seeking
peace and comfort.

Shrunk down deep and still into a corner,
covered up silently to disappear.
Woke to heavy footsteps everywhere—
police searchin'
for a runaway,
but I was sleeping safely tucked away.

And now…
I'm grounded,
probably grounded for life.

Caged

How you gonna ask me,
"Are you being harmed,"
in the room with the one harming me?

Ask if I "feel safe"
while sitting in the very place
I feel stretched thin
and trampled like lace.

Scared, unrested for days,
hungry, unfed,
and clearly afraid.
Had to make you step with me
outside this place
and tell you the horrors
alone—
within these walls
I faced.

Training you to understand
how to properly inquire
about "safe."

That room in there
is my cage.

Toy

Wind me up and watch me go
 as my energy dwindles
 my battery runs low-
 as my little wind up motor can no longer go.

Feed me from the flame of your lies
 Promises to love, keep, cherish all die.
 The fuel for my love time, run time, play time-
 derived from your promises of us to be.

Wind me up and watch me,
 As this girl topples over on the floor-
 My heart was his little wind up toy.

I Heard

I hear you speaking about me.
I guess you didn't see I was standing right beside you
when your words choked out my want to breathe.
A foster child, you say—
"She's not worth an ounce of your time.
I knew kids like her before, they left on the drop of a dime.
She'll use you, you'll drop your guard,
then she'll leave and where will you be?"

I heard you.
  You know, I'm listening—
  but I told you what your heart was missing.
I never asked for this life.
Y'all walk 'round here questioning,
  never asking what my story is,
  never trying to understand more than the gist.
I'm no heroine or protagonist.

Why blame, why assassinate, why mislabel me?
This was the life that someone else's actions chose for me.
Can you hear—
or are you turning a deaf ear to me?
Why should I be turned away,
  rejected, dejected, subjected to warped beliefs of you?
You didn't hesitate to even hear me out, boo.
If I had a say, I'd never leave.

In my shoes,
  the only decision in this life for me is –breathe.
  I had no say in the mistakes,
  the heartache,
  my foundation quakes,
    destruction left in my mother's wake.

No say in what placements terminate,
or why my mom didn't choose her children to exterminate.

I am a child just like you, but my worries run steep.
I'm weary of making promises I intend to keep,
prepared always in case at a new stranger's I'll have to sleep.
But dislike me or hate me,
I won't retaliate.
My existence here's not up for debate.

Hunger for Love

I hunger for your love
for your touch, your kiss
for the way you smile
the way you laugh
for the little things that make you you.

I hunger for the sound of your voice
for the words you speak
for the comfort they bring

I hunger for the closeness
the safety of your arms
the beating of your heart.

I hunger for your love
with every breath I take
with every thought I make
I hunger–
for love.

Shadow Tells a Story

I tried to run, a fugitive fleeing from a distant land,
but still the shadows found me.
They whisper a haunting story,
a chilling tale—
one of love and lies,
heartache, betrayal, abandonment,
enslavement and neglect.

A child's voice, unbowed barely unbroken,
speaks where others fall silent.
Her life, a string of disappointments,
a path paved with letdowns.
Hands meant to guide her only held her back,
words meant to brighten her day instead struck her down.

Left by the man who planted the seed,
abandoned by the woman who bore her in pain,
blessed with eyes that produced tears in vain—
she buried her past like a dog hides a bone,
built a house atop it,
and left it alone.

But then a woman came—
tore the house down to the ground.
From the cracks and shattered glass
slipped the secrets she had tried to keep buried.
Words like daggers, sharp and precise,
pierced her heart with venom.

She tumbled into the abyss
until she thought she found love.

Every day was like summer,
drenched in passion and heat.
She danced in the sun,
smelled the rosebuds,
and thought love was the flame on the candle of life.
She blinked—
and when she opened her eyes, it was gone.

In darkness she resolved to climb,
mountains of books her foothold,
chapters her rope.
She absorbed knowledge,
slaved for grades,
hoped they would someday pay her way.
Yet beneath the honors and ribbons,
she found herself bound, gagged,
ensnared by her own goals.

Happiness dwindled,
joy wandered astray,
and she realized her very existence was riddled with holes.

Lowering her eyes against the world's glare,
she thought herself plain,
simple, unremarkable.
She wondered: what prize is worth losing your soul
When once abundant time doled?

Still she longed to reach out,
different from the rest,
not hiding behind a plaster mask.
But she failed to see the tears she could not cry,
the truth behind the lies.

She tried to flee like a gazelle from a lion,
to hide like a deer from the hunter.
But still the shadows danced around her feet,

telling her story for all to hear.

And when the sun finally rose across her sky,
she lifted her head high,
back straight, heart unchained.
Her tale, chilling and scarred,
was carved into the road she walked—
yet still she rose like dust,
Unashamed. Unafraid.

Give it a title

A title—that is the directive.
Yet, how does one categorize an errant thought?

It is akin to a dream, entangled and elusive,
a transient utterance, a nascent idea,
a lost echo, a vanished trace,
a delicate entity, displaced.

Thus, I present it herein without appellation,
a fragmented artifact, a delicate structure.
Nevertheless, it communicates
authentically, despite its anonymity—
whatever its essence, it is offered to you.

Mask

Glitter and ethereal feathers,
affixed by invisible adhesive.
Each plume sways with a delicate grace,
an illusion of effortless joy and captivation.
You present a vision of enchanting artifice to the world.

Beneath that meticulously crafted, smiling facade
Your authentic self resides.
Passerbyers claiming a small fragment of your expressions
affection, admiration, for the radiant image presented
It's all superficial admiration,
none truly comprehend the vulnerable essence
Of full you.

Carefully constructed guise radiating brilliance
light in this unforgiving,
shield against its harsh realities
 a beacon,
Warding off solitude's delights.
A poignant question lingers
 in the silent spaces of your heart–
who will love you when you're bare,
Or genuinely embrace you when you dare
Present in your full authenticity?

To embrace the you beyond
Shimmers and plumes woven into public identity
Behind performance and projection,
 Resides there a raw, vulnerable soul
A brightness holding eyes weeping in solitude–
 longing to be seen, understood, and cherished true,
presenting its unvarnished form.

Stole, from me

Knife to my neck—
Outnumbered
hands pressed hard on my head.
I only went along with yous;
I feared being dead.

Knife to my neck,
you said you'd make me disappear.
If I spoke out about this,
you'd harm the sister I hold so dear.

Slashed out my hope,
all my spirit broke.
I cried out for help to her;
she saw me and acted
like you were playing a joke.

Knife to my neck,
his hands on my back.
I never asked to burden this—
no adults, just regretful existence.

BACKSTABBED

Sister—
I thought a sister you'd be,
but you blame me and say,
"Here's where you shouldn't sleep."

You left a blemish on my sleeve,
a dark stain where my heart used to be.

You chose yourself –my dearest– and strangers,
overlooked bloodlines, sister ties.
Shadow turned against me
like an unexpected tide.

You left me no safe ground,
no place loving for words to confide.

Sister
I thought a sister you'd be,
but you chose perversion
and strangers over me.

In Bondage

When did my mind become a prison—
When did the cell door close, locking me behind these four walls?

Was it when I didn't decide?
When I didn't make up my mind
 to speak up for my own needs,
 to make my voice heard in the midst of the chaos,
 to bring into the light my foolish and selfish deeds?

Was it all a matter of my heart
which encased me in this dungeon—
filled with the putrid stagnant air of past exhales?
Struggling to find new breath, new hope, new light,
to win my way out of this darkness
I scraped the ground beneath me.
Somehow I was determined to find the key
to release me from my personal hell.

My mental sight was blanketed
by a vast forest of black trees,
my knees rested on a floor covered with dead leaves.
Strangely I found myself in a new place,
yet, I was still unable to find my sight.

"My Heart! My Heart!" — I wept,
 "Have I given it away?
 My Love! My Love!
 Where has it gone astray?"

On my knees, still on my knees,
forever I found myself kneeling,
praying—

begging—
for a new beginning to the end
I could not see ahead.
 For new light.

Warped Family

I was trying to stand–
socks slipped and a hand grazed
I apologized.
A child confused and dazed.
There was a gleam in your eye.

Touching and pulling and forcing
where brotherly hands shouldn't be.
I said enough.
I said no.

You set fire to the bed while–
where I sleep.
You told me it was me or my dearest—
threats of harm whenever I sleep peaks.

Still no one in this warped family chooses;
blindness of belief, no one to protect me.
This is not how family is supposed to be.

ME?

Uncried tears,
unfaced fears,
untied fates—
rescue shown up late.
Crushed in this moment,
screams in vain.

Is this name even my name?
My birthday even my day?
Have I ever made a real friend?
Is my life real or pretend?

Nothing here belongs to me;
real hurts done to my body,
invisible child
no one chooses to see.

Caseworkers,
county workers,
rushing through
to check me off—

have me questioning,
pondering deep—

Am I real?
Who is me?

Bathroom Brushes

A child with a mother
but no mothering.
She never has the things she needs—
her hair undone,
her emotions a wreck,
her mother's anger forever unchecked.
No love or joy draped
over shoulders or neck.

Let's meet in the bathroom before class.
I'll brush your hair,
wipe your tears.
I'll listen—
it's no heavy ask.

I have extra pins
and ponytail holders.
I hear you,
I see you;
for your pain
I'll be a shareholder.

I hope we stay connected
when older,
but even if there's absence,
please know you'll be missed.

I hope to remember your face
and moments forged
in this place.

TRASH BAG QUEEN

Picked up, told, "you've minutes to prepare."
Quickly, grabbed some things —
Then swiftly disappear.
How dare they put my clothes in a jumbled pile,
A trash-riddled mess that mocked me all the while.

The way I've been treated —
Call me the Trash Bag Queen,
Carrying all I had in broken seams.
This scent will never die, to me.

TWISTED

She walked all over me,
trampled over my senses.
No consequences held—
trotted on my boundaries,
sat me deeper in the trenches.
I paired her with people
who a friend to her could be—
friends who used to be mine,
no longer remembering
friendship with me.
A priority was she to me,
a sister I'd always wanted—
but her mother pitted us against,
and our bond was affronted.
Now only competition she sees.
She devalued and defaced
this sister in me—
sinister and twisted,
trying to sell
this flesh on me.
Her mother and her
only price tags
on my flesh
did see.

Hit Me

Pushed me—
over bed,
over table.
Threatened to stab me,
to leave me marked,
scarred,
or disabled.
Pushed her mother,
threatened my stride—
all because I told
on her predator
and tried to preserve
their family pride.
Standing against her,
for her,
strong—
she told me
I'd be unalived.
How am I your enemy
when protection
was my only goal?
I guess I have to let
this placement unfold—
hit me,
and hate me
if that is your goal.

Down Eyes

You labeled me a liar, but I told the truth.
Took me and discarded me downstream—
silenced before speaking, children and youth.
I told them how you took our brother,
made him frequent prostitutes;
when his fingers on young bodies lingered,
I brought concerns to you—
you laughed.
You claimed I wanted and asked for
mistreatment at the hands of a brother.
Cut off all ties to counselors;
caseworkers dropped every ball,
excused his wrongs unnumbered times.
Labeled me an instigator,
told me I wanted to be misused.
Threatened to turn me out too—
Kensington Avenue.
You said I was big enough to be grabbed,
grown enough for grown men to have.
911 dismissed my pleas as prank calls.
Proof that blood was never thicker than water—
cursed, I was never meant to be anyone's daughter.
Finally, benefits under threat, you dropped me—
silenced before speaking, children and youth.
I told them to go back
and save my sisters from your abuse.

I'm beginning to believe
using my voice carries no use.

Let's See

They told me a family is what I deserve.
No one even knows who I am;
no one listens to what I say.
Whoever thought there'd come a day
where "deserve" and "family"
in a sentence for me would be said?
Too many placements,
unremembered voices,
unkept promises—
broken.
No one wants me
unless as food token,
but sing sweet lies
of loving
and wanting to keep,
until intentions of their heart
I see.
Sure—are you sure?
A family I deserve…
but whose agenda
will it serve?
Emancipate me—
level this out
and let me be.
I doubt there's a family
deserving of me
in this broken.

I'm only a burden
of responsibility
in this broken.
Go ahead—
let's see.

Uneasily Demised?

They mocked the light they could not see,
dismissed the brilliance and beauty.
Yet she endured with dignity,
a faith that would not compromise,
a steady flame, uneasily demised?

She chose to mother, strong, alone,
without a spouse to share the road.
Through ridicule her courage shone;
her love became the only home—
a fortress built from heart and bone.

Love, she taught, is not always kind:
austere, exact, not yet refined
by trials sharpened, never swerved.
It lingers, faithful, unconfined—
by the Spirit of God sublimed.

Littest Page

Am I the marker for loss and death?
I said we should visit,
but was ignored before your final breath.
I love you—
loved you—
but I couldn't cry for you,
solemn, breathless goodbye.
I couldn't muster up a single tear
for a grandfather I held so dear.
Traveled with the littlest page
through storms of anguish,
trains filled with rage—
traveled on tracks no sadness spilled,
though sanity this life has milled.
Still,
I didn't shed a tear for you.
Instead the distance of Virginia
spread thinning between
my running stride,
to my eyes
your memorial unseen.
I hope I can remember you.

Breathless

Sometimes I feel starved of breath, feeling starved of death,

like silence pressing on my chest, sorrow putting me to test.

Tear drops drown me because of youth,

distance swallows what I've left—refuse to bow to burdened health,

yet somehow I'm reminded I'll make it through.

My Plea

Lord, hear my plea, my soul laid bare,
I need your mercy, I need your care.
I've wandered far, I've lost my way,
but still I kneel to You and pray.

Forgive the times I turned aside,
forgive my doubt, forgive my pride.
Restore my heart, renew my song,
and keep me in Your love lifelong.

Author's Note: This embedded haiku appears as an isolated layer within the poem, reflecting its inner core.

Flicker

I close my eyes and *wander* back,
down a *long* and
faded track.

Moments flicker, shadows *play*,
ghosts of laughter
far away.

Time has *stolen*, yet I keep,
these reminiscences
buried deep.

Their Rocking Robin

So bright, but something is amiss:
her posture, hair change, eye twitch,
loss of balance,
random silences, and tremors.

I see them, though she disguises.
I hear gentle but firm, comforting tones,
soft, loving, reassuring lies,
minimizing her pain and concern
to comfort the hearts of the dearly loved.

But I see it lingering above her love—
a cloud:
fear of abandoned love and empty nest.

Stylishly beautiful in red,
she gives her parade.
Rockin' Robin, singing and dancing along,
each moment shared, little Robin rocking along.

I pray for more encounters
to join with and dance to your song,
joyfully grieving, yet still jovial in tune.

Liminal

Not here, not there,
not in between—
heartbeat and palms befuddled.

Learning to lean into new titles
of being.
To be in this moment,
to understand this—
unromantic, yet still longing,
awe-inspired amazement
at the wonder of your gifts.

Tunes hummed behind lips
while hands strummed,
lost in admiration
of the beauty of you—
just as you exist, here.

I'm unsure how this new
connects,
how many misinterpretations
label any link.

But truest is:
spirited friend,
I recognize inherently
your mourning song.

Raccoon's Goodbye

She gifted her son the kissing hand,
lived with honor, authority, and gentle grace.
The knowledge and kindness she exuded,
steps soft as royalty's child.

She told of fun times,
tough times,
ends and losses.

Now eyes around the corners kiss darkness,
the silence and weight of thinned time—
awe-encompassing.
I know she's leaving us soon.

Raccoon eyes and paws, dark in mourning,
but she shines freely, unchained to body.
As kissing hands and raccoon cries
croon on and lullaby last goodbye.

Bright Eyes

You are so bright-eyed and beautiful—
reserved, but a story yet unfolded,
blue-green, surprised by the way you
see me,
hear me,
here me.

You don't have to apologize;
I want to hear you out.

She hurt you, but you didn't deserve it.
She walked out on her beautiful gifts.
I know that made you angry—
don't let the anger
ball up emotional fists.

No child deserves a mother
who won't honestly put forward face.
I apologize she left you unmothered;
heal up for future emotional blows.

You are loved—
kindred spirit leaning toward me,
who thought equal flame,
a strong conversation,
would bring to me.

I hope we'll stay friends forever,
regardless if either of us
move about.

Sublime

It started with a button—
unordinary,
yet it kept us tethered
in a world that wanted unfastening.

We picnicked under bridges like trolls,
crumbs falling into stories
shared of hopes;
the shadows cool,
the air humming its malatonic tune—
out of key,
but unforgettably ours.

We walked until streets turned trails,
endlessly linking into forever sky.
Every step was a dare,
every glance,
a secret compass.

Passion invited
but safety-harnessed,
draped in respect—
every spark mindful
and curiously examined
not to burn
hands holding hands.

And there,
in the oddness of us—
button,
bridges,
laughter in strange places—
something sublime
rose quietly,

as if the world itself paused
to admire
the cautions
and fullness
as we traverse gently.

Tell me your story again.

Lost Passion

Passion—
 once a flame burning fierce and high,
 now an ember smoldering low,
 barely alive.

I remember the days when desire consumed me,
 when love sang loudly, bright and strong.
 But time and trial have worn it thin,
 and silence lingers where fire once belonged.

Now emptiness echoes in the place of song,
 and I search for sparks, for light, for fire—
 a reason to feel,
 a way to inspire.

Yet hope remains, a spark concealed,
 hidden deep but not repealed.
 Waiting still to be revealed—
 a flame to rise, a love restored,
 a passion rekindled once ignored.

Will I find me?

I wonder if I will ever find me—
heavy-laden, not born a fair maiden,
a missing child no one is searching for.

I wonder—will I ever find me?
All the pieces of childhood scattered,
memories wisped away.

Tormented by nightmares of what I went through:
locked doors, bathroom corners, torn clothes,
the strange, gentle welcome of strangers.

I have no home. How can so many mistreat me?
Don't they see? No one even cares to look.

I have searched high and low—outside and within—
and still I am my only loyal friend.

Tossed aside like trash, eyes lightless as flameless ash;
still no one bothers to ask:
Will I ever find me?

Recollection

Memories unflood like waves to shore,
faces I've loved, voices no more.
I try to hold them, but they fade,
like shadows cast at close of day.

Recollection bittersweet,
the past and present rarely meet.
Still I treasure what has been,
those fleeting moments carved within.

Inescape

Watching me from far away,
I feel your eyes, they always stay.

In the shadows, in the light,
you haunt my days, you steal my night.

I can't escape, I can't be free,
your gaze has taken hold of me.

A captive soul, I cannot hide,
from eyes that follow, open wide.

Author's Note: The haiku's contradiction is deliberate; it reflects the duality of abuse written in 2009 for National Domestic Violence Awareness Month.

Unfair Trade

It was not you—
    that wasted me
        the cyclic silence
    And hours poured
           into an empty chalice.
    Not your breath,
Only time spent in vain.
  Unnoticed was the teasing
        rumors of love deserved.

Done trading time for scraps
      Left emaciated by–
    dishonesty and illusions.

Control Is Not Love

When I reached back for old hands,
for foster family, for friends—
she erupted.
Rage to cut every tie,
to prove I belonged only to her.
Control dressed as care.

They said my brain was wrong,
that I was too used to fighting.
But I never called it fighting.
It was existence.
Existence that burned.
Why live to be beaten,
abandoned,
claimed only to be broken again?

I remembered God—
a prayer whispered young,
before I could read a Bible,
before I could name His shape.
Others laughed,
thought I spoke to air.
He answers and is real.

She taught me
love means cutting you down,
calling you broken,
doubting your memories and experiences.
Existing on the approvals of those harming you
Abandoning any sense of self or independence.
love means making you choose
between her and everyone before or after.

But control is not love.
It is theft.
It is fear.
It is the hand that cages you
and calls the cage home.
It is exasperation of the broken.

They tried to twist me into believing it.
But I know better.
Love does not sever.
Love does not strangle.
Love does not need to be proven
by erasing what came before.

I will not let control define love.
I will not carry their twisted gospel.
I have learned—
real love expands.
It holds without choking
It frees.

Author's Note: This triptych written in 2008, "The Storm" is presented as a three-part poem. Each section reflects a different stage in the traumatic cycle: the lived experience of crisis (full poem), the fragmented nature of traumatic memory (plain text), and the quiet aftermath of survival (italicized). These three movements are meant to be read together—as a progression, a disorientation, and ultimately a re-emergence and was written during my exploratory stages of written expression.

The Storm

Troubles flow *over my heart*
like a breeze *over raging waters—*
taking pieces *of my soul with it,*
like the sand *swept away*
by the current of *the ocean.*

Lightning cracks *across my sky,*
thunder shakes *my core inside.*

But this storm *is no passing rain.*
It howls *like a hurricane,*
ripping roofs *from every shelter I built,*
tearing apart *the fragile walls*
I thought *could keep me safe.*

It twists *like a tornado,*
lifting me *high only to slam me down,*
uprooting *what was thought anchored*
scattering *my memories like debris,*
turning *familiar streets*
into unrecognizable *wreckage.*

It crashes *like a tsunami,*
a wall *of water swallowing my voice,*
drowning *the prayers I try to shout,*
dragging *me beneath waves of fear*
so heavy *I forget how to breathe.*

And still,
after devastation,
after loss,
after silence *grips the broken ground—*
the *sky begins to clear.*

Calm *will come,*
even *to this.*
The waters *will recede,*
the winds *will die,*
and light *will break through*
the ruins of *my night.*

The storm *will* fade,
but I—
I will remain,
forever changed,
yet still standing

Not a Dream

This is not a dream—
   I know it by the echo of my own scream,
   ricocheting off the mirrored walls,
   chasing me in circles
   through a funhouse I cannot leave.
The pain is real—
    it cuts, it bleeds, it stays.
   Every corner hides a reflection,
   each one wears my face,
   each one carries the scars clear and seen.
The night returns again, again—
   a carousel of shadows,
   round and round,
   the same fear painted new each time.
Fear wearing my own shape
   I close my eyes,
   but still the floor tilts,
   the laughter distorts,
   and the loud terror does not sleep
   No waking from this endless fight.
   The morning sun refuses me.
The light is swallowed whole
   by walls that bend but never break,
   by footsteps that chase but never catch.
   This is not a dream—
   I bawl
   the walls only answer back with silence,
   hush that knows my name.
Still I live.
  I inhale.
  I stumble through the labyrinth.
  This nightmare spins me
  through its own rhythmic screams,
  No—
  This is not a dream.

Quake

Through the nights of endless fear,
        I longed for someone to hold me near.
Through the days of weary stride,
I only wished you by my side.

The storm winds rose, the shadows stayed,
        and tides pulled harder every day.
I reached for you but was found by the void,
silence storms could not destroy.

The ground screams—
        tearing apart the dream.
The streets split, cars swallowed whole
Dwellings engulfed by earth before dawn.

I stood on the edge of broken,
        watching the earth devour in deep inhale.
Earth gave way beneath me pale,
A still cry, *I need you near*—
unanswered.

Your absence echoed louder than,
        every aftershock a hollow ache.
And though I stand to fight,
I fell apart without guiding light.

Through ruins, dust, and fractured skies,
        the plea the question why: Remains–
I sought for you in quake and tide,
but I was left
no one,
None by my side.

Hollow Child

Close those eyes and wander back
down corridors where dust takes breath.
Shadows hang like heavy drapes,
silence stretches—
a hollow weight.

His giggle, light and sharp,
skipping across the broken.
Tiny feet race down the hall,
leave no prints, so sound befalls.

Then slowly roll
circle the room to dance
without light
He echoes of a lullaby
off-key, too loud
in the empty air.

Laughter silent—
how unusual
with empty endless.
let your voice howl like a cracked moon call
bouncing off bare walls,
happy haunting energy trapped in between.

Reach and stretch,
this silence indulging your breath
The air thick with memory's death,
traces of laughter
imagine you in fullness.

Time a burglar,
Fights to keep,
this recollection buried deep:
a playful child

in an unlit room,
where joy exists alongside gloom.

Tangent Maze

Thoughts unravel,
past zero's hour.
Logic fades,
dreams take power.

One thought becomes another—
memory,
wound,
prayer half-muttered.

Memory feeds ache,
ache supplies longing,
longing nurtures fear.

I circle–
stumble,
traverse
give chase to my own reverberation.

What breaks the maze,
but carries pain-
drags into Despair?
Despair discovers then stows away a spark-
Hope.

She leans into what broke the maze.
Round and round—
these thoughts sojourn
tangle, knot,
Enmeshed in flesh,
thread uncut.

Sleep won't come.
It teases at the fringe,
then slips away before it's grasped.

Night devours the edge of day.
watches shadows eaten by light,

uncertain—
was it Hope that survived
or Despair that learned
a new song?

Author's Note:
"Generations One Dream" is a poem written in 2006 during 8th grade and edited the same year. The original poem (under different title) was submitted for a Martin Luther King Jr. Day writing contest for the Boys and Girls club of Easton, and counted for a class assignment. It was awarded first place. The following poem is centered on a juxtaposition of the teachings of both Dr. Martin Luther King Jr. and Langston Hughes.

Generations, One Dream

Langston and Martin…
   Both kings of dark hues
   resonate with me,
   but I see in their lives,
   regardless of age and experience
   My goals can still be reached with hard work.

These men of different times
   yet connected in civil pleas—
   aims to redirect the misguided
   and thwart a nation in unrest,
   in youth both fearful of dreams festered and dried,
   laid out deferred,
   to recognize others by character, not skin tone.

Where they both sing
   of the weary blues
   and simply heavenly tunes
   I have a dream too, have you heard?
   I dream to play tambourines to glory,
   to live this life not without laughter.

I have already spent a lifetime
   laughing to keep from crying,
   but if you saw what I see
   you'd be asking,
   "Don't you want to be free?"

Even if, when at the mountaintop,
   I may not be there to speak
   in the languages of the brave
   and tired of being oppressed,
   the riot of the other America
   teaching it wide
   until inequality is gone.

One day I hope to see—
   both their dreams alive,
   breathing,
   unencumbered
   and free.

First Race XC

You wouldn't let me quit
even through injury—
you told me teams stick together.

You wouldn't let me quit,
even when there was no joy,
even though I wasn't the fastest
or even falling mid-heat—
because I made a commitment.

Seven days a week to practice,
rain, snow, sleet, or shine.
I trained each day
and weight lifted the most—
still I fell behind.

Asthmatic flares,
pollen and fresh-cut grass in the air,
inhalers to the ready—
and airs of doubt spoken out loud
from those who said they love me.

You encouraged me to run,
lectured me to keep my pace.

Then during my race—
you interrupted me
and ran over to hug me,
could have gotten me disqualified.

I joked it off, but you told me
I was so slow
it was as if I wasn't even in the race at all.

I gave it my every effort,
 painful bruises on arms, legs, and thigh.
I didn't quit,
 finished dead last—
 but I did it with pure grit.

I'm proud of me.

Perfection

I've heard I have high expectations of me,
but not to be perfect—just to enjoy learning.
I want to be good at whatever I do;
wouldn't you?

If I become a doctor with scalpel in hand,
I want my patients to trust me.
If I am a lawyer or judge holding true the law,
I want the victims to trust my motives, dedication.
If I choose the Airforce or Navy,
if in missions abroad,
whatever I become to bring praise to God.
I want to be the most knowledgeable on hand.

I don't want to be a settler of sorts
or jack of all trades.
I also don't put in hard work to get praise.
I just want to be me—
the best version of me.
I want to be great at whatever I do.

I am sporty, but I'm told I'm not female enough.
I shrink down, hold my tongue…
still told I make too much sound.
I excel and crush academic strides
and get told top 10% is laughable and a joke.

I won a writing competition,
sing till heart's content—
but my joy snuffed out as soon as heaven sent.

Compared, pushed down, told to comply,
  told love will never come
  without makeup on my eye.
Told my friends were all failures and beneath me—
  severed,
  cutting a flower off before it blooms.
The criticism flung at me
  is what family words intended to do.

No matter where I go,
  what I do—
  I will never be perfect,
  neither will any of you.
Maybe less judgmental standards
  would help you feel accepted too.

Family

No family is perfect—
some ties are meant to be broken
before the bond irreversibly harms you.

Some families will dictate,
some harm and turn their backs on you.
No family is perfect,
even the ones who choose.

Love is not certain
and endearment is not sure—
but when a family is devoted,
that family endures.

Push through the wreckage,
work through the pain.
Hold on to joy;
don't let misunderstandings
drive you insane.

Growing, I've moved to and fro–
Never truly knew a mother,
Not quite fitting a daughter's role
unsure where I'd go.
This world and myself a mystery–
can't recall dissipated memories.

But you embraced me here,
having never mothered anyone
arms rough and rugged.
I don't know you well
and you don't know me—

and while your love, although jagged
here, feels somewhat like home to me.

Consistent and assured
 you promised to be—
 you show up,
 you respond,
 engage willingly.

I'm unsure what makes family
 while no ties bond us here.

But you're family I love;
 I pray you too
 don't soon disappear.

Celebrated

A cake baked just for me—
not just one but a whole three.
Presents and a familiar tune…
who knew a birthday could be
joyful.

Stayed in one place long enough
to make connections,
while she allowed me to see
others close to heart.

I can tell their attendance
is bittersweet,
but she put on a smile for me.

She tried cooking things
she's never done
and stood with me
while I learned in the fire too.

I'm sorry if flames unknown from me
seer your sleeve.

Finally a celebration
with family—
who'd have believed.

Capsized

A storm threw me overboard—
below calm, into the raging sea,
an ocean of dread and willful ignorance.
Water replacing air in me.

The raft adrift,
floating, pulled just out of reach.
Isn't there anyone searching for me?

Drowning—
sinking into dark,
cold and deep.

Capsized in the ocean of gloom,
pain perpetuated,
unsavable in this typhoon,
reaching for safety—
rescue to come soon.

Depleted

My body ached,
my eyes burned,
head feeling light—
bustling and rolling through papers
for more than a week,
no life.
I've eaten little
and slept less.
My mind empty,
I cried for days,
filled with the sorrow of loss.
Finally wet eyes—
my creativity had died,
my voice lost,
desires gone.
I cried for the loss
of my voice.
My skin shows signs
of stress rash,
hair's begun
to fall out again.
Stress so high a level
there is nothing left
of me to do.
I feel broken inside.
I'm lost—
and there's nothing
I can do.

BREAKING

I watched
I listened
I witnessed
I wept
heartbroken by promises unkept.

Alone,
unwanted,
unhomed,
abandoned
astonished at the wounds unseen.

Between
unheard
displeased
absurd
absorbed by the hollow tide.

I felt my fears, wounds open wide.

Unmothered

I've been told I "can't be a woman"
Seeing no one raised the woman in me.
I "can't be a mother…
When no one mothered my inner me."
I'll "never measure up or down"
To whomever decided with borrowed crown.
Sold when told I am "unlovable by design,"
Unmothered, far from divine.

Who made you my judge?
Who gave you permission to drag me through
And through the mud?
Not my Creator — not me.

Come here — Blind, and you will see,
Your words only stun temporarily.
Unmothered though I be —
I love unbothered,
Stand unjustly judged,
Others' actions chose this life for me.

If You Survived Trauma Please know–

Healing has no fixed pace.
Some wounds take weeks; others take a lifetime.
But there *is* a future that belongs to you.
You are not alone.

If you need support:
U.S.: Call or text **988**
International: iasp.info/crisis-centres-helplines/

ABOUT THE AUTHOR

Shanita Menso is a faith-based Marriage and Family Therapist with specialization in trauma recovery, crisis intervention, and high-conflict family systems, as well as an author whose work is shaped by lived experience and a commitment to breaking generational cycles. She lived formative years as a foster child then was adopted in late adolescence. Growing up navigating rejection, instability, and emotional wounds later fueled her calling to walk with others through their own storms. Her clinical focus includes intergenerational trauma, high-conflict family systems, and faith-integrated healing. Before entering the mental health field, Shanita supported families facing cognitive decline, grief, and long-term illness, experiences that deepened her compassion and sharpened her intuition. Today she is a devoted wife and mother whose writing—especially *The Breaking*—flows from a faith-centered belief that healing is possible, cycles can be broken, and generational wounds can be identified, treated, and prevented from taking root in the next generation.

www.ingramcontent.com/pod-product-compliance
Lightning Source LLC
LaVergne TN
LVHW021714080426
835510LV00010B/1000